Dedication

This book is dedicated to my dearest children, Teddy, Nora and Astrid. May God's Word always be in your heart.

"But the fruit of the Spirit is love, joy, peace, patience, kindness, goodness, faithfulness, gentleness and self-control...."Galatians 5:22-23 (ESV)

Taken from Holy Bible English Standard Version

Love

When God is in my heart, He will show me how to love people.

Love is being patient and kind. Love is not rude, self seeking or proud. Love has hope. Love never ends and it never fails.

When I show people love, they will see God's Spirit living inside of me.

Joy

When God is in my heart, He is my joy.

God is always with me, whether I am playing alone or with my friends. God loves me just the way that I am. Thanking God brings joy to my heart.

When I am joyful, people will see God's Spirit living inside of me.

Peace

When God is in my heart, He is my peace.

When too much is happening, when a room is too noisy, when I get upset or argue. These are moments I can turn to God and pray for His peace.

When I am peaceful, people will see God's Spirit living inside of me.

Patience

When God is in my heart, He will help me to be patient.

Waiting in a long queue for the swing. Feeling hungry and knowing that dinner is still not ready. These are moments I can turn to God and pray for His patience.

When I show patience, people will see God's Spirit living inside of me.

Kindness

When God is in my heart, He will show me how to be kind.

Treating others the way I would like to be treated. Sharing my toys. Saying nice words. Listening to people, are all kind things to do.

When I show kindness, people will see God's Spirit living inside of me.

KINDNESS

Goodness

When God is in my heart, He will show me how to be good.

Using good words like please and thank you. Helping tidy up after playing with toys. Letting others go first, are all good things to do.

When I show goodness, people will see God's Spirit living inside of me.

Faithfulness

When God is in my heart, He will help me to have faith.

Going to church. Spending time praying. Speaking to God. Trusting God's Word, are things I do to keep my faith.

When I have faith people will see God's Spirit living inside of me.

FAITHFULNESS

Gentleness

When God is in my heart, He will show me how to be gentle.

Playing calmly with a toy. Being pleasant with pets, babies, family and friends. Considering how someone may feel, are gentle things to do.

When I show gentleness, people will see God's Spirit living inside of me.

GENTLENESS

Self-Control

When God is in my heart, He will teach me to have self-control.

Listening and obeying rules. Not eating all the cookies in the jar. Turning anger into positive energy, are all acts of self-control.

When I show self-control, people will see God's Spirit living inside of me.

A prayer for you

I pray that God's Fruit of the Spirit grows in me everyday. In Jesus Name. Amen.

Galatians 5:22-23

The Fruits of the Spirit are:

Made in the USA
Coppell, TX
30 May 2023

17518864R00017